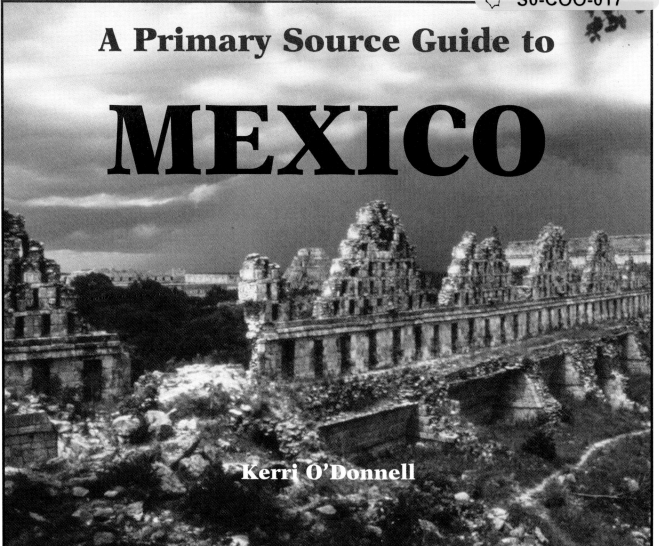

A Primary Source Guide to
MEXICO

Kerri O'Donnell

ROSEN CLASSROOM
PRIMARYSOURCE

Rosen Classroom Books & Materials

New York

Published in 2004 by The Rosen Publishing Group, Inc.
29 East 21st Street, New York, NY 10010

Book Design: Haley Wilson

Photo Credits: Cover, p. 1 © The Image Bank; p. 4 (map) © Map Resources; p. 4 (inset) © Danny Lehman/ Corbis; p. 6 © Kevin Schafer/Corbis; p. 8 © Archivo Iconografico, S.A./Corbis; p. 8 (inset) © The Bridgeman Art Library; pp. 10 (General Santa Anna), 18 © Bettmann/Corbis; p. 10 (inset) © D. Boone/Corbis; p. 12 © Galen Rowell/Corbis; p. 12 (inset) © Charlie & Josette Lenars/Corbis; p. 13 © Dave G. Houser/Corbis; p. 14 © Macduff Everton/Corbis; p. 15 © Jack Fields/Corbis; p. 16 © Reuters NewMedia Inc./Corbis; p. 20 © Randy Faris/Corbis; p. 22 © EyeWire.

Library of Congress Cataloging-in-Publication Data

O'Donnell, Kerri, 1972-
  A primary source guide to Mexico / author, Kerri O'Donnell.
      p. cm.
Includes index.
  ISBN: 0-8239-6592-9 (library binding)
  ISBN: 0-8239-8076-6 (pbk.)
  6-pack ISBN: 0-8239-8083-9
  1. Mexico—Juvenile literature. [1. Mexico.] I. Title.
  F1208.5 .O36 2004
  972—dc21

                                2002004167

Manufactured in the United States of America

Contents

4

The Country of Mexico

Mexico is a North American country that lies just south of the United States. Mexico shares its northern border with the states of California, Arizona, New Mexico, and Texas. A river named the Rio Grande, or "Large River," makes up about two-thirds of the border between the United States and Mexico.

Mexico has the third largest population of all the countries in the Western **Hemisphere**. Only the United States and Brazil have more people. About one-quarter of Mexico's people live on farms or in tiny villages. The rest of Mexico's people live in larger towns and cities.

◀ El Monumento de la Independencia, or the Monument of Independence, is a well-known symbol of Mexico's freedom. It is in Mexico's capital, Mexico City. The people of Mexico City call the monument "the Angel."

A Varied Landscape

Mexico has many different kinds of land. About two-thirds of Mexico is covered by mountains and high, flat land. Mexico also has deserts, plains, green valleys, and rain forests.

Northern Mexico gets little rain and is made up mostly of deserts. Not many people live in this area because few crops can grow there. Most people live in southern Mexico, which gets more rain and can support more crops. A part of southeastern Mexico gets a lot of rain. Mexico's rain forests are found there.

There are three large mountain ranges in Mexico. One is in the east, one is in the west, and one is in the south. All three ranges are called the Sierra Madre, which is Spanish for the "Mother Range."

Native Empires and Spanish Rule

The first Mexicans were Native Americans who came from the north more than 10,000 years ago. More than 2,000 years ago, great Native American **civilizations** began to develop. The people built **pyramids** to honor their gods. They also created a calendar, a system of writing, and a counting system.

In the 1400s, the Aztecs built Mexico's last Native American **empire**. Spanish explorers began to arrive in Mexico in 1517 and soon went to war with the Aztecs. Within a few years, the Spanish had defeated the Aztecs. Spain ruled Mexico for the next 300 years.

◄ The stone on this page is an Aztec calendar that was carved in 1479. It weighs about 3 tons (2.72 metric tons) and is about 12 feet (3.66 meters) wide. The drawing is from a 1581 Spanish manuscript. It shows an Aztec man watching in a treetop as a Spanish ship reaches the Mexican coast.

General Santa Anna

The Alamo

10

An Independent Country

Mexico won its independence from Spain in 1821. One of the heroes of Mexico's war for independence, General Santa Anna, was elected president in 1833. The next year, Santa Anna decided Mexico was not ready for **democracy** and made himself **dictator**. Santa Anna led Mexico in many battles over land with the United States.

Today, Mexico's government is a democracy. It works a lot like the United States government. Mexico's leader is a president, and a congress makes the country's laws. Both the president and congress are chosen by the Mexican people.

◀ When Santa Anna became president, Mexico included Texas. In 1836, Santa Anna's army defeated Texas soldiers at the Alamo in San Antonio. Texas gained its independence soon after. After almost ten years as an independent country, Texas became part of the United States in 1846.

Mayan writing on ancient building

The Mexican Economy

Mexico's economy depends heavily on farming. Corn is the country's largest crop, but many kinds of fruits and vegetables are also grown there. Coffee, cocoa beans, cotton, and wheat are also grown in Mexico. These crops are sold to different countries, including the United States.

Mining and manufacturing are also very important to the Mexican economy. Mexico has many valuable

minerals and is the largest producer of silver in the world. Mexico is also a leading producer of oil.

Millions of tourists come to Mexico each year and spend billions of dollars. Many tourists visit the ancient pyramids and other buildings of southeastern Mexico. Others visit the beautiful beaches along Mexico's coasts.

The People of Mexico

Most Mexican people are mestizos, which means that they have a mixture of **ancestors**, usually Native American and Spanish. Most Mexicans speak Spanish. Some also speak the languages of their Native American ancestors.

Family is a very important part of Mexican life. Several **generations** of a family may live in the same

house, and they usually eat their meals together. A typical Mexican meal includes tortillas, a type of flat bread made from ground corn or wheat flour. Tortillas can be filled with meat, cheese, or beans.

◄ For hundreds of years, the Mexican people have built their towns and cities around public squares that the Spanish called plazas. Today, almost every village, town, and city in Mexico has a plaza where people meet to talk with friends and family.

Fiesta!

Mexico celebrates holidays with fiestas, or **festivals**. Mexico's biggest festival is Independence Day, which is on September 16. The Mexican people celebrate their freedom from Spain on this day. The festival actually begins on the evening of September 15 and includes colorful decorations, fireworks, special foods, music, and parades.

Religion is an important part of Mexican life. Most Mexicans are Catholic, a religion that the Spanish brought to Mexico in the 1500s. Mexico celebrates many religious holidays throughout the year.

◀ On September 15 in Mexico, the president stands on a balcony of the National Palace in Mexico City and rings a historic bell. He shouts "Mexicans, long live Mexico!" The people gathered in the *Zócalo*, or main square, shout back *"Viva!"* which means "Hurrah!"

The Art of Mexico

Mexican art has a long history. Ancient Native Americans decorated their huge pyramids with religious paintings, carvings, and stone figures. Weaving was also an ancient Native American art. Today, some Mexican people still make beautiful handwoven cloth and baskets.

The Spanish built many churches when they ruled Mexico. The walls of the churches were also covered with religious paintings and carvings.

One of Mexico's most famous painters was Diego Rivera. He was known for his simple, brightly colored paintings of Mexican life and history.

◀ Diego Rivera liked to paint murals in public places. Murals are large paintings that often cover entire walls. Rivera wanted to share his ideas about Mexico's history, culture, and political problems with the Mexican people.

Mexico Today

Since the mid-1900s, Mexico has increased the amount of products it makes and sells to other countries. However, many Mexicans still lead hard lives. Some farmers don't have the tools they need and earn little money. Others have moved to cities to find jobs. Many Mexican cities are very crowded.

In 1993, Mexico, the United States, and Canada all signed a treaty to increase trade among their  countries. In the years to come, Mexicans hope this treaty will strengthen Mexico's economy and lead to better lives for its people.

This view of "the Angel" at left shows a busy day in Mexico City. The 200-peso note above shows a portrait of Sor Juana, a Mexican nun who lived from about 1648 to 1695. She had become well known for her religious poetry by the time she was eight years old.

Mexico at a Glance

Population: About 100,000,000

Capital City: Mexico City (population about 20,000,000)

Official Name: Estados Unidos Mexicanos (United Mexican States)

National Anthem: "Himno Nacional de Mexico" ("National Anthem of Mexico")

Land Area: 756,066 square miles (1,958,202 square kilometers)

Government: Democracy

Language: Spanish

Unit of Money: Peso

Flag: Mexico's flag was adopted in 1821. The green stands for independence, the white for religion, and the red for union. At the center is the country's **coat of arms**, an eagle eating a serpent.

Glossary

ancestor (AN-ses-tuhr) A member of your family who lived before you.

civilization (sih-vuh-luh-ZAY-shun) The way of life followed by the people of a certain time and place.

coat of arms (COAT UV ARMS) A shield shape with blocks of color and pictures. It stands for a country or a person.

democracy (dih-MAH-kruh-see) A government run by the people.

dictator (DIK-tay-tuhr) A ruler who has total power over the people.

empire (EM-pire) A group of nations or states under the rule of one leader or government.

festival (FES-tuh-vuhl) A time of feasting or celebrating, usually to honor a special event.

generation (jeh-nuh-RAY-shun) People in a family who are about the same age. Parents are one generation, and their children are another.

hemisphere (HEH-muh-sfeer) One half of Earth.

mineral (MIH-nuh-ruhl) Something found in soil that is not an animal, plant, or other living thing.

pyramid (PEER-uh-mid) A building with a square base and four sloping sides that meet in a point at the top.

Index

Primary Source List

Cover. Mayan ruins at Uxmal. This photograph shows a building commonly called House of the Doves at Uxmal, built between about 600 A.D. and 900 A.D.

Page 8. Aztec carved calendar stone, ca. 1479. Now in the Museum of Anthropology, Mexico City.

Page 8 (inset). Drawing from 1581 Spanish manuscript. This image comes from a history of the Aztecs written in 1581 by Dominican monk Diego Duran, who lived and worked among the Aztecs. The original manuscript, called the Codice Duran, is in Spain's Biblioteca Nacional in Madrid.

Page 10. Portrait of General Santa Anna. This portrait of Santa Anna, painted by Paul L'Ouvrier around 1858, is now in the Henry Luce III Center of the New-York Historical Society in New York City.

Page 10 (inset). The Alamo. The church is all that remains of the mission built in 1718. The curved top above the door is not part of the original building but was added in a reconstruction in 1850.

Page 12. Mayan pyramid. The photograph shows a pyramid commonly called El Castillo pyramid in the Mayan ruins at Chichen Itza, on the Yucatan peninsula of Mexico. The pyramid was probably built before 800 A.D.

Page 12 (inset). Mayan glyphs, ca. 600 A.D.–700 A.D. Yaxchilan, Mexico.

Page 14. Mexican plaza and church. The photograph shows the central plaza, or *Zócalo*, of Mexico City, built in the 1500s by Spanish conquistadors on the site of the Great Temple of the Aztecs, which they had destroyed. The huge Metropolitan Cathedral was begun around the same time but was not completed until the 1900s.

Page 18. Photograph of Diego Rivera, 1944.

Page 21. Mexican pesos. Shown here are the nuevo (new) pesos issued by Mexico in 1993 to replace the old pesos. One new peso equals 1,000 old pesos.

Web Sites

Due to the changing nature of Internet links, The Rosen Publishing Group, Inc. has developed an on-line list of Web sites related to the subjects of this book. This site is updated regularly. Please use this link to access the list:
http://www.powerkidslinks.com/pswc/psme/